A JOURNEY OF DISCOVERY THROUGH BIG BLUE

This book is dedicated to all the
people who have helped shape our
beautiful journey of discovery.

A Journey of Discovery Through Big Blue
Copyright © 2021 by Alexandra Macare

All rights reserved. No part of this publication may be reproduced,
distributed, or transmitted in any form or by any means, including
photocopying, recording, or other electronic or mechanical methods,
without the prior written permission of the author, except in the
case of brief quotations embodied in critical reviews and certain
other non-commercial uses permitted by copyright law.

Tellwell Talent
www.tellwell.ca

ISBN
978-0-2288-5281-0 (Paperback)

CONTENTS

CHAPTER 1
BACKGROUND AND BEGINNING 1
   Distribution Policy 2
   Introduction 3
   Let's Dive In 5
   Maps and Timeline 6

CHAPTER 2
SEA CREATURES 8
   Iguanas 8
   Yellow Tube Sponge 10
   Brain Coral 14
   Sea Turtles 18
   Whelk 22
   Crabs 26
   Black Triggerfish 30
   Upside-down Jellyfish 32
   Ballyhoo 36
   Other Sea Creatures We Encountered 38

CHAPTER 3
ACTIONS WE TOOK..44
- Weekly Plastic Reduction Data................................44
- Plastic Reduction Phases..46
- Beach Clean Ups and Data.......................................47
- Things You Can Do..49
- Visualizing and Comparing......................................50
- Cladogram and Connection.....................................52

CHAPTER 4
MORE TO KNOW...54
- References...55
- Resources..56
- Glossary...58
- About the Authors..60
- Special Contributors..63
- Pictures We Took...64
- More Poetry from Us..70

CHAPTER 1
BACKGROUND AND BEGINNING

DISTRIBUTION POLICY

We are a group of learners viewing ourselves as global citizens, caring about life on Earth. We prefer you to read this book digitally because our distribution policy is to minimize printed copies and help send recycled copies to children who would benefit. We hope when you read this book you will be inspired to make your own journey of discovery through life.

INTRODUCTION

You may be wondering what isy! stands for. It is the acronym for our school name International Sustainable Youth. Our school is really unique for many reasons. One, is because the approach to learning is a process created and practiced by our school leader, Alexandra Macare. We learn by what she calls 'process based learning' using real world experiences and projects, in other words, learning for life. Another reason is we travel all over the world! We have projects and classes everywhere we go. Our school is always changing and shifting places with every new project, in 2020 that was 5 places!, In each new place we have a new class, like the one formed here in Providenciales, SMB Kids Academy Commission. SMB is another acronym we used to identify the last initial of our school members in Turks and Caicos. S is for the name Soni, M is for Madan and Macare, and B is for Bhushan and Benevento. We have traveled to many places: Singapore, Brazil, California, Panama and Boracay, and now we are in Turks and Caicos.! All our projects have one thing in common, we are learning about the world and how we can make it a better place.

LET'S DIVE IN

Here we go on our journey of discovery through Big Blue with you. We're excited to learn and change with you. We started this journey all coming from different places: USA, UAE, and Brazil and joined here in Providenciales, to learn about the ocean.

As we researched for this book, we went on many expeditions and studied lots of people. Some people we encountered in our learning journey include, Sylvia Earl, Amanda Gorman, Walt Whitman, David Attenborough and Anna Du. Amanda Gorman recited her poetry at the inauguration of Joe Biden, and we were inspired! We linked our studies to Walt Whitman and read many poems he wrote. All our learning gave us the idea to express what we were discovering, through poetry.

We created a timeline to help us organize the sequence of important events and people as we learned. The one we created in school was really big and detailed, too much for the book, so we made a smaller one to share. Can you add your own special events to the timeline? You can use a rules to help you measure and mark special dates. Maybe you can make your own timeline!

Look at our time line and see if you can answer some questions. How many months did Walt Whitman live? In which century was the first scuba suit made? When was Sylvia Earle born? Who was born in the year closest to the year in which you were born? Do you know what a gyre is? How many gyres are on the map? Do you know what the black dots on the map are?

MAPS AND TIMELINE

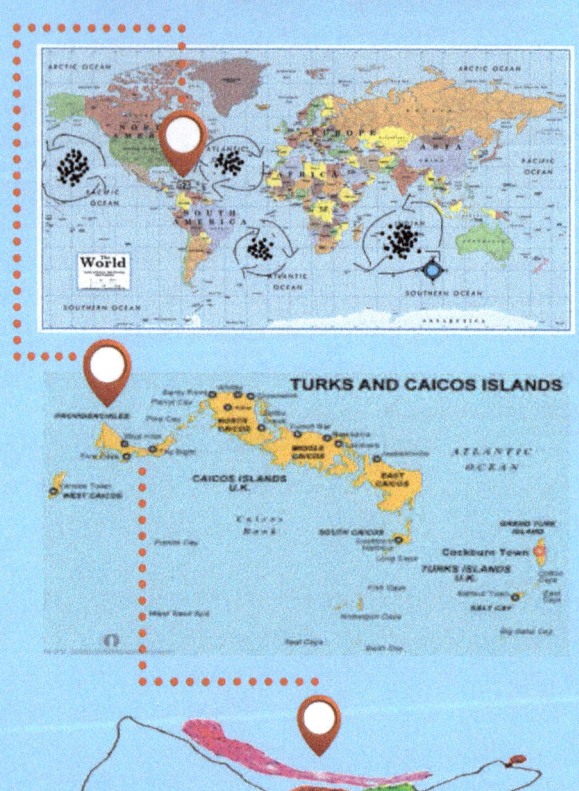

- Rising Tide tours
- Sun Sea and Sand
- White Villas
- Brise De Mer Beach Villas
- Shambhala
- Bight Reef
- Smiths Reef
- Turks and Caicos Barrier Reef

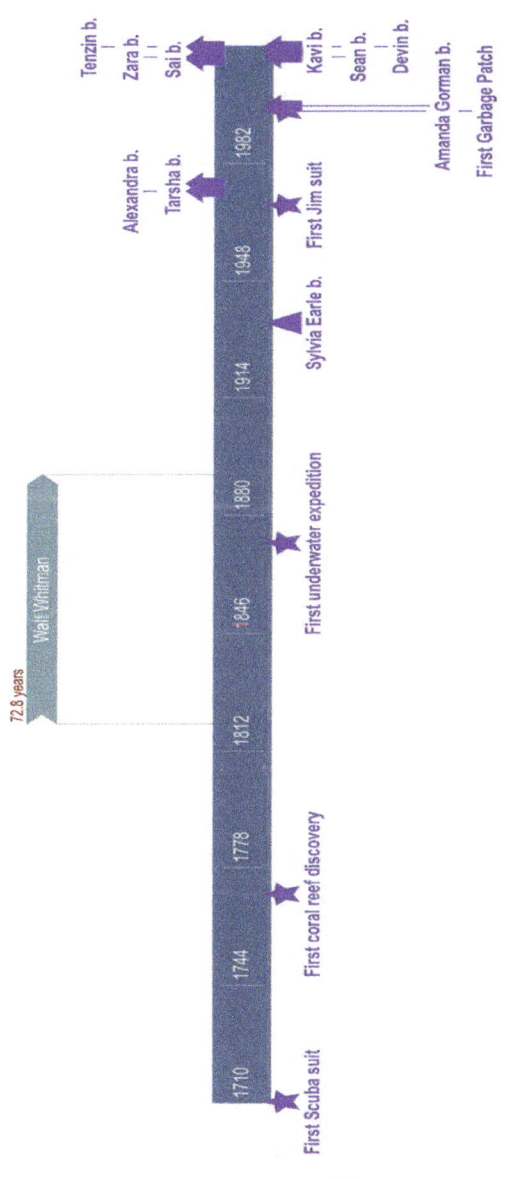

CHAPTER 2
SEA CREATURES

Hi my name is Devin Madan. I was born in 2015. In my study about the ocean, I learned about Iguanas. Iguanas, like the Rock Iguanas of Turks and Caicos, live near the coast. They are very good climbers and fast runners, but they are endangered. Only 5% of Rock Iguanas remain! From my learning experience, I know how important it is for humans to protect Iguanas. Iguanas are hunted by many predators like dogs and cats brought to the island by people. Their population is going down and they can die from pollution. Iguanas eat seaweed and it can contain plastics. Plastic can go in the seaweed if humans litter and trash goes into the sea. Over time, the plastic breaks down and turns into microplastics. Do you know what microplastics are? Microplastics are tiny bits of plastic. The microplastics can get caught in the seaweed that the iguanas eat.

To save them, always recycle plastic and avoid plastic as much as possible. Whenever you see plastic in the environment pick it up and recycle it.

FUN FACT: Iguanas puff up so predators don't attack.

FASCINATING FACT: A group of Iguanas is called a mess or a slaughter.

FAST FACT: the Spiny Tailed Iguana is the fastest running lizard.

Iguanas are really
good climbers and so fast I hope
thinks species will last
I think they are the coolest
reptile
when I see them they
make me smile

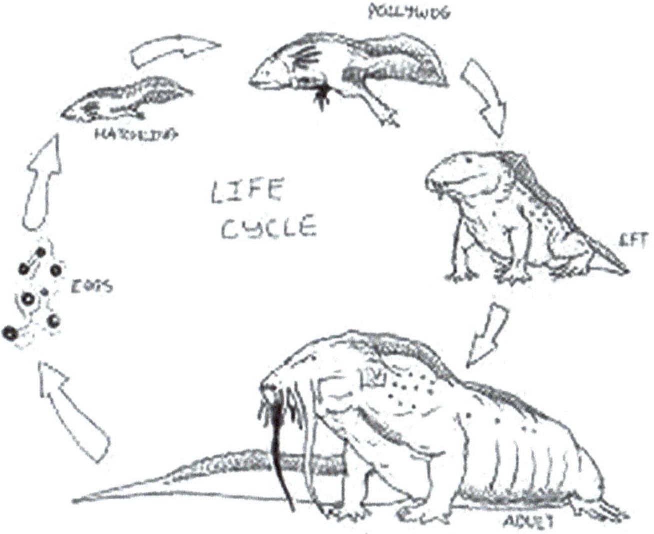

Hi my name is Tenzin, I was born in 2014. I came to Turks and Caicos with my family and joined SMB Kids Academy to help write a book about the troubles in the ocean. In my study of the ocean, I learned about the Yellow Tube Sponge. One of the things I learned is that the Yellow Tube sponge is an invertebrate. Do you know what an invertebrate is?

Yellow Tube Sponges eat food particles which they suck into their holes. They blow the water waste out of the big hole on the top called the osculum. They are sessile, like all sponges, and they're unable to move.

From my learning experience, I know how important it is for humans to stop littering the ocean. It is also important for humans to protect the ocean and the Yellow Tube Sponge, because the Yellow Tube Sponge is an important part of the ocean ecosystem. Scientists don't know a lot about the Yellow Tube Sponge but they do know they produce antimicrobials, which may help us in the future. What do you know about antimicrobials? How might they help us?

Yellow Tube sponges can do cool things that we can learn from, like when one is knocked over the cells can rearrange themselves to create a new vertical tube! How do they do that?

I think we could do a lot to protect the ocean. By the way, another cool fact is Yellow Tube Sponges can reproduce in two ways. One way is for it to break off and the broken pieces will grow a new sponge! The other way is by male sponges squirting out sperm that swim and float down into the female sponge and then the fertilized eggs are squirted out of the osculum and then float down to the ocean floor and start to grow a new one!

Taxonomic ranking of a Yellow Tube Sponge
Domain: Eukaryota
Kingdom: Animalia
Phylum: Porifera
Class: Demospongiae
Order: Verongida
Family: Aplysiidae
Genus: Aplysina
Species: Yellow Tube Sponge

Below you will see the other way
Yellow Tube Sponges can reproduce.

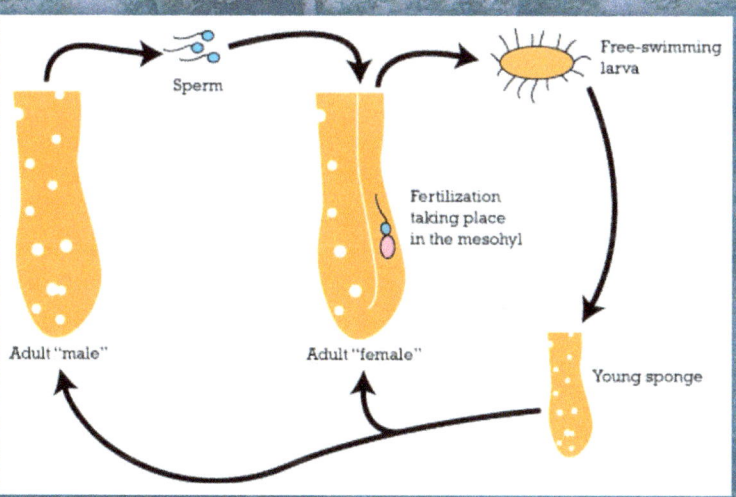

By: Tenzin Soni

The yellow tube sponge was very still

And the very black sky of stars was full

Yet it looks happy but I feel emotional

Maybe the sponge is unaware but I know the ocean is in trouble

FUN FACT:

Yellow Tube Sponges may have been around for as many as 500 million years!

Ocean Joke:

What did the ocean say to shore?
Nothing, it just waved Get it?

Hi, my name is Kavi Bhushan. I was born in 2014. When we wrote this book I was 6 years old. My school came to Providenciales and we made a class called SMB Kids Academy Commission. We started a project to learn about life in the ocean. In my study about oceans, I learned about the kinds of corals in the Caribbean Sea near where I was staying for a couple of months. I also looked at the coral reefs in the Atlantic Ocean. I got to go snorkelling and see many corals, one was the Brain Coral, it looks just like a brain! They are found in shallow warm-waters all over the world's reefs. Let's look at the food chain below. If the Brain Corals' population goes down, they can not filter, feed and eat small zooplankton. So a lot of Fish Fry may lose their primary food source, and not only Fish Fry but a lot more stuff might die. From my learning, I know we need to protect the coral reefs. Some things I am doing to help are reducing my plastic use, spreading the word about how to keep corals safe by doing things like not touching them, cleaning up trash on the beach, and encouraging others to recycle. I hope that if we keep the oceans clean, the reefs will live and more fish will have homes.

FUN FACT: 1 human touch can cause the death of an entire colony Oils from your skin will disturb the delicate mucous membranes which protect animals and corals from other diseases, so do not touch corals, or else more and more will die.

FRANTIC FACT: plastic can rip open holes into corals.

FRANTIC FACT: 50 percent of all coral reefs have died in the last 30 years. 😟

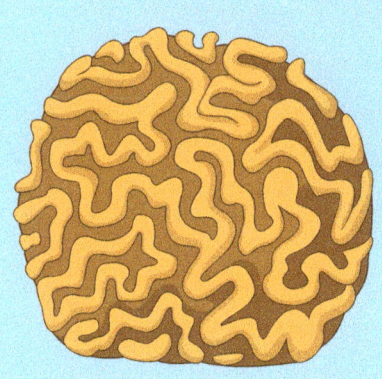

Time to dive into—Joke Time! What do fish sing during winter? Christmas corals!

Let's look at the taxonomic ranking too.
Domain - Eukaryote
Kingdom - Animalia
Phylum - Cnidaria
Class - Sea anemones/Anthozoa
Order - Hexacorallia
Family - Alcyonacea
Genes - Acropora
Species - Can you guess?

Brains in the coral
How smart can you be? Let us share the cool coral reef.
All the care in the sea,
Let's help the ocean stay and b

— Kavi

Hi! 😊 My name is Zara. In my study about the ocean, I learned about Sea Turtles.

From my learning journey, I know how important it is for humans to protect Sea Turtles. If sea turtles have no home many bad things can happen. To explain what I mean, here are some examples. Let's imagine that sea turtles are absent in the food chain, wait... let me give you a mini explanation: Green Sea Turtles eat a lot of seagrass and seaweed which grows on the ocean floor.

> Turtle Joke! What do you call a famous turtle? A shellebrity!

The seagrass is also home to a lot of marine life like seahorses and prawns; and it's also a breeding ground for fish and a LOT more sea creatures. Ok, we need to keep the turtles alive because they eat the dead ends off the seagrass and if they are gone, that might not happen. And then the seagrass may continue dying and then the fish cannot breed there, or the seahorses and prawns, basically all the animals cannot live there.

Sea Turtles are important to the ecosystem because they eat and poop a lot. They break down some of the plants that they eat into protein. But, sea turtles, like the Green Sea Turtles I studied, are becoming endangered and that's resulting in fewer eggs being laid and that means fewer nutrients for the beach. Most beaches have a pretty fragile ecosystem in that they don't get many sources of nutrients so there is very little vegetation. Sea turtles help support their ecosystem when they nest. Do you know how? Well, of the tens of thousands of eggs that are deposited by the turtles, some won't hatch. The eggs that don't hatch will decay and help the beaches with nutrition. With lowering turtle populations, fewer eggs are deposited and this could result in less vegetation and this may contribute to beach erosion! Some people are even stealing turtle eggs!! Can you believe it? This is also lowering the turtle population.

Sea turtles also die from getting tangled in nets and choking on plastic garbage that people litter. So, I'm going to tell you a couple of things I have done to help stop this. I am not going to tell you everything that I am doing, because it's really a lot, but I will tell you some. My family has a lot of friends here in Turks and Caicos. So, we contacted the TCI recycling company to find out how we can recycle. We got a bin and have been collecting every week. We also compost! 😊

TAXONOMIC RANKING OF A GREEN SEA TURTLE

Domain: Eukaryota
Kingdom: Animalia
Phylum: Chordata
Class: Reptilia
Order: Testudines
Family: Cheloniidae
Genus: Chelonia
Species: Chelonia mydas

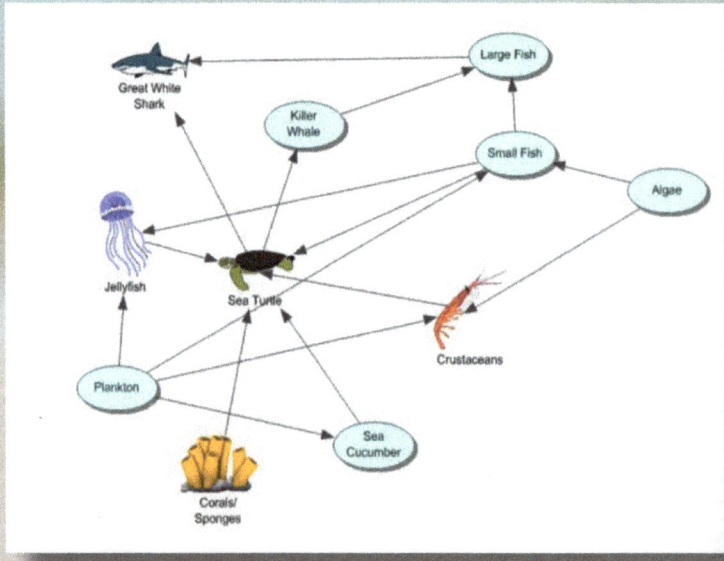

Sea turtle oh Sea turtle
Swimming in the sea
by the mangroves and me.
You look so sturdy,
Not at all frail,
as you swim by me
like a boat with a sail.

Hi, my name is Sean Madan. I am eight years old and I was born in 2012. I came to Turks and Caicos to study the ocean! When the SMB KIDS ACADEMY -- MY class-- went on an expedition and we saw lots of Whelk and then I said to myself, "Hey, I really don't know a lot about that." So I decided to research them and one thing I found was that whelk eat other mollusks and little fish, which was very surprising to me. Another thing I found was that there are over 50 species of whelk! When I found these facts I still didn't know why I should care about whelk. One day later, I found that if we don't protect the whelk population then bad things could happen. Imagine, if the whelk goes from the food chain then the limpet population may go up and eat most of the sea grass. If that happens, then the sea turtle population may go down!!! How? You may wonder how the seagrass affects the turtle population: this is because turtles feed on and breed in seagrass. I started to see how everything was connected and why saving one creature helped save others. We've learned that the purpose is not only to help us, but to help other people and save animal lives. Some things we are doing to achieve this goal are-producing a book about the ocean that is very exciting. We also held beach cleanups and we might hold more. Each week we try to reuse, reduce and recycle. We weigh our plastic weekly because we want to see if the weight is going down by using less plastic.check out our page that shows the data about our plastic reduction.!

FUN FACT FOR FOODIES:
did you know that whelk is
a fairly healthy seafood
option since it is high
in protein and vitamin
B12 and low in fat?
However, like
other shellfish
whelk is also high
in cholesterol.
(a butter sauce
or a trip in the
deep-fryer adds
fat and calories.)

INTERESTING FACT:
did you know that
some people incorrectly
call or mistake
whelk for conch?

Domain	Eukaryote
Kingdom	Animalia
Phylum	Mollusca
Class	Gastropoda
Order	Neogastropoda
Family	Melongenidae
Genus	Busycon
Species	Knobbed Whelk

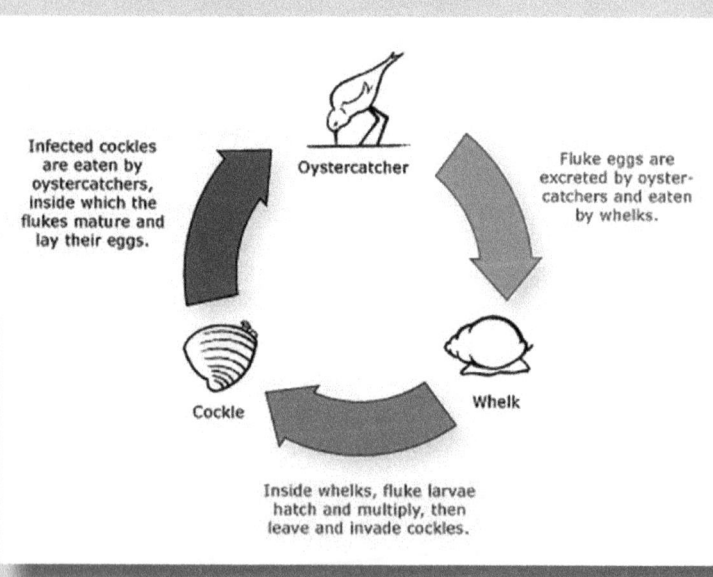

Here is a poem I made about the whelk!!!---

Hello everyone, I'm a whelk right here,
but from me you have nothing to fear.
I may look big or small,
but if you are a fan of turtles
I am right with y'all.
We share the coral reef comunity
and help take care of the plants in the sea
and that just means we are all one family.
I may look gray, but I just want to say
that we all have light inside us.

Hi, I am **Sai Bhushan**. I was born in 2011. We came to Turks and Caicos with a purpose in mind, it was to study the ocean. When my school went on an expedition I saw a crab. I realized how much I did not know about **Crabs**. So, I decided that I wanted to study it. In my study about crabs I learned many things. For example, crabs are decapods (10 feet). Even though most crabs live for 2 - 3 years some can live for up to 100 years! Crabs can exert up to 350 kilograms of force, that is enough to lift 60 pounds. Do you know how much is 60 pounds in kilograms? I discovered so much from crabs and why it is so important to preserve crabs. Unfortunately, crabs mistake plastic for food and shells. This makes them buoyant. Do you know what buoyant means? If a crab floats it cannot hunt so it dies of starvation. If crabs die out, the mussel and limpet population might explode which could cause a massive decline in seaweed. Seaweed is a breeding ground for many animals so this would ripple through the food web and leave it in chaos. This would not just be contained in the ocean because seaweed stops beach erosion. If seaweed populations decline, beaches would erode faster than ever. If we lower the amount of plastic we use we can help save crabs. One of the things my school is doing is using less plastic and recycling the rest. You can do the same and help prevent a crabtastrophe.

Below is the food web and taxonomic ranking of the crab.

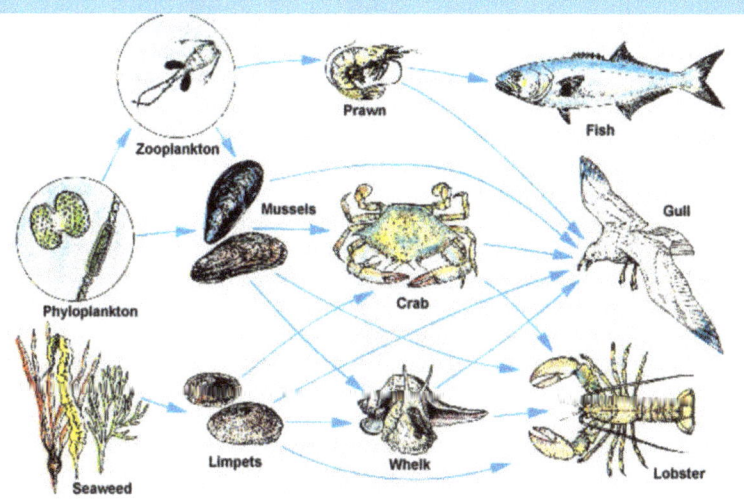

Domain	Eucaryote
Kindom	Animalia
Phylum	Arthropods
Class	Malacostrancans
Order	Decapods
Family	Brachyura/Crab

Poem

Crabs you might not be aware
Of what is happening
but I know and I care
Oh crab you are so strong
too bad you do not have a song
oh crab you are so fast
I wonder how long you can last

Hey... It's me, Zara from the sea turtle page, you may recall, page 18. Anyway, I also learned about the Black Triggerfish, AKA the Black Durgon. From my experience, I know how important it is to protect Black Triggerfish and their habitat.

Most triggerfish species are attractive fish and some species have become super popular. Fishermen fish for the triggerfish because people want them for their aquariums. This has caused the fishermen to fish for more triggerfish even though they are a threatened species, lowering their population in the wild. Scientists are working on trying to reproduce the triggerfish that are already in aquariums, and leave the wild triggerfish ALONE!! The triggerfish have cool ways to catch their prey. They dig out prey like crabs and worms by flapping away debris with their fins and sandblasting with water squirted from their mouths! Triggerfish also use their quite tough teeth and jaws to take on sea urchins, flipping them over to get at their bellies, which have fewer spines. Triggerfish leave so much food in their wake that small, smaller fish will follow and feast on the leftovers.

These beautiful fish like to hang out alone unless the moon or tides draw them in for a social gathering. During certain moon phases and tides, they like to spawn. In some species, the boys have a whole harem of females. Do you know what that means? It means they might have hundreds!!!

Now, before I go, I am going to show you the taxonomic ranking of the Black Triggerfish

Right down here...

Domain: Eukaryote
Kingdom: Animalia
Phylum: Chordata
Class: Actinopterygii
Order: Tetraodontiformes
Family: Balistidae
Genus: Melichthys
Species: M. Niger

So, I got to go now, sea you later!! lol

Lifecycle of a Fish

Hey, welcome back, you might remember me- Sean -from the whelk page!! This time, in my study about the ocean, I learned about the Upside Down Jellyfish. A group of jellyfish, like the Upside Down Jellyfish is called a bloom, swarm or a SMACK!!! Another thing I learned was that they have 360 degree vision!!! A third fact I learned was that climate change has a smaller affect on jellies compared to other animals.

From my learning experience I know how important it is for humans to protect the Upside Down Jellyfish. If they have no home (they can live in lakes, the mangroves and ocean) then many things can result. For example, if the Upside Down Jellyfish are absent in the food chain then other things like the crustacean population, which they prey on, may increase.

WOBBLY FACT: Jellyfish are 98% water so when they wash ashore they evaporate!!!

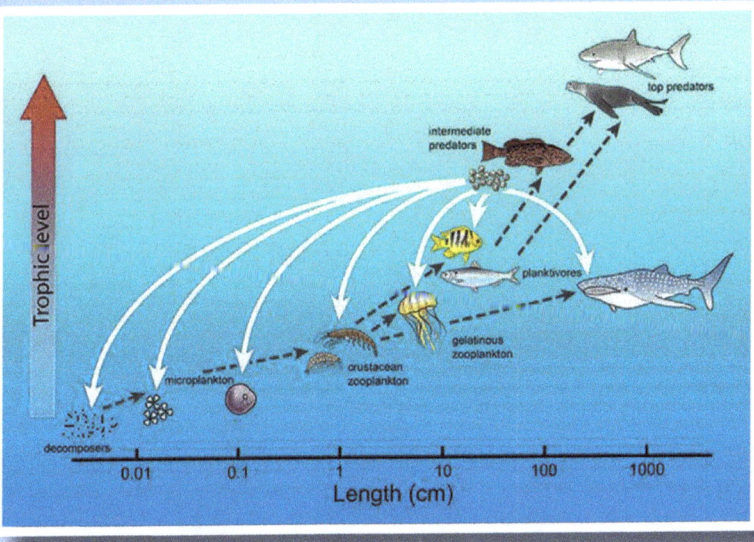

One thing I am doing to help is using less plastic so that it won't go into the ocean. This affects them because crustaceans are known to carry traces of microplastic which may go into the body of the jellyfish and cause them to die. The Upside Down Jellyfish is a big part of the food chain because if they disappear from the food chain then the sunfish and whale sharks may have to eat other sea creatures and this could disrupt the food chain.

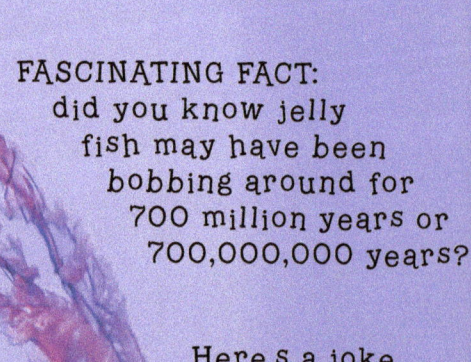

FASCINATING FACT:
did you know jelly
fish may have been
bobbing around for
700 million years or
700,000,000 years?

Here's a joke
about jellyfish:
What do you
call a jellyfish
on a plane?
A flighto
plankton.

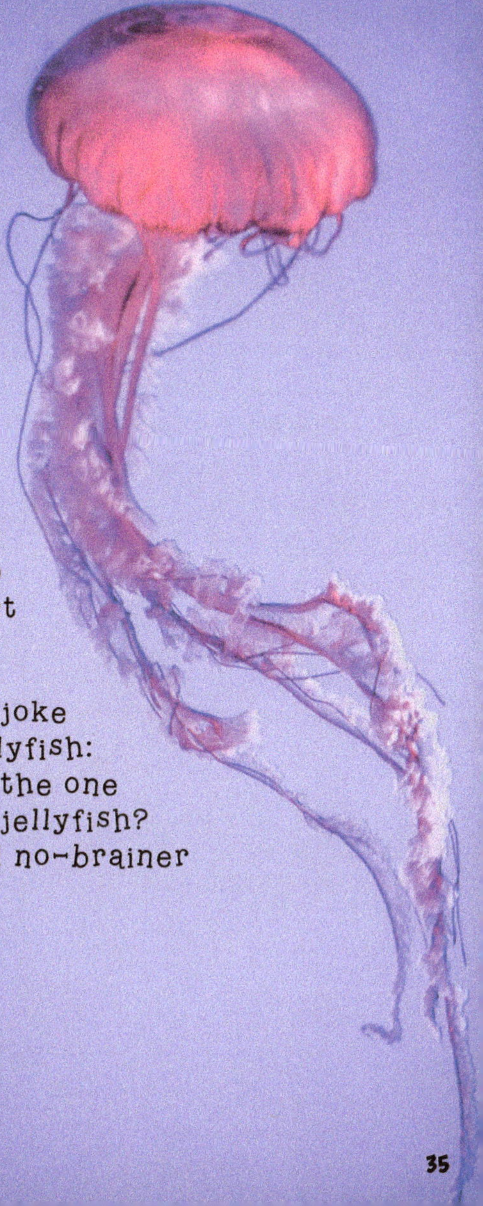

DISGUSTING
FACT: They have
multiple mouths
and they poop
out of the same
body parts
as the eating
body parts.

GROSS FACT: No
brain or heart

Here's a joke
about jellyfish:
Have you heard the one
about the jellyfish?
A real no-brainer

Hi I am Sai. You might remember me from the crab page. I want to share some cool facts about the Ballyhoo fish. Let's dive in.

The Ballyhoo fish is bait fish meaning it is used to catch other fish. It can grow up to 55 centimeters. The Ballyhoo are omnivores. Do you know what an omnivore is? It means that they can eat both animals and plants. They are known to travel in schools and feed on algae, seagrass, plankton, decapods, copepods, and smaller fish.

I have learned a lot from Ballyhoo. Even though the Ballyhoo are plentiful now, if we do not preserve them they could be overfished. Because the Ballyhoo is a bait fish, it feeds many animals. So, if its population goes down the populations of the animals that feed on them could go down. We can all help protect fish from overfishing by being consensus consumers and knowing where the fish we eat come from.

FAST FACT: The Ballyhoo fish is known to have caused ciguatera poisoning, a kind of poisoning caused by eating reef fish whose skin contains certain toxins, in humans.

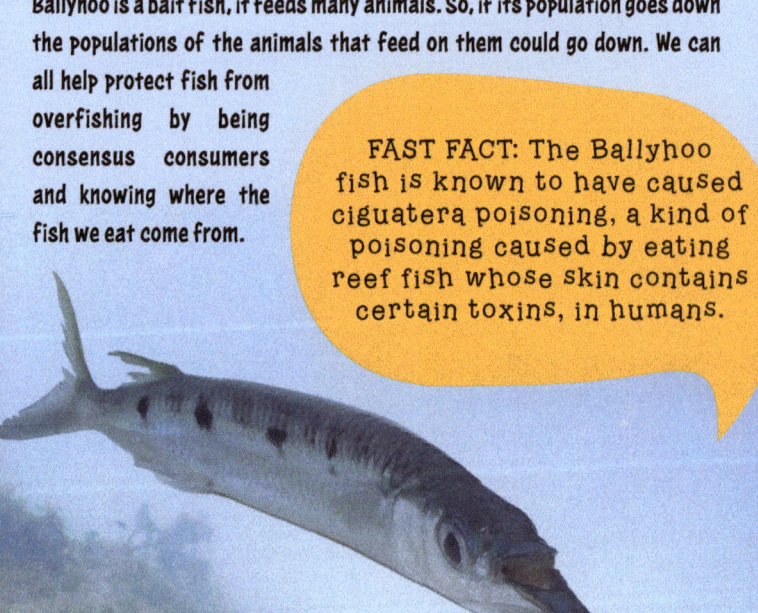

Domain	Eucaryote
Kindom	Animalia
Phylum	Chordata
Class	Actinopterygii
Order	Beloniformes
Family	Hemiramphidae
Genus	Hemiramphus
Species	Hemiramphus brasiliensis/Ballyhoo

Above this text is the taxonomic ranking of the Ballyhoo.

P1-Knock knock.
P2-Who is there?
P1 The Bally.
P2-The Bally who?
P1-I m Ballyhoo.
P2-No, who is Bally?.
P1 No, I am the Ballyhoo.
P2- Bally WHO????

OTHER SEA CREATURES WE ENCOUNTERED

Extra Sea Creatures We Encountered in our journey. We found them all fascinating and hope you do too!

Sai here again, this time to tell you about the
Green Razorfish
Green Razorfish "hide" by curling up, if this does not work it will dive into the sand. They are between 2.5 and 4 inches long and swim between 5 and 35 feet deep.

Hi, it's me Kavi from the Brain Coral page.
Another one of the sea creatures we encountered is the
Blue Carpet Anemone.

Fun Fact: The Blue Carpet Anemone can sting with its tentacles, it's important for your safety and theirs, that you do not touch them.

Also Here Is a Picture of The Carpet Anemone.

Hi, it's Devin and I love Stingrays. They use something called the ampullae of Lorenzini to see. It feels the electric charge of the prey when it swims close. They don't use their eyes to look for their prey but they have them on the top of their heads.)

1. The largest species of stingray measure 6.5 feet in length and can weigh up to 790 pounds.
2. Stingrays are closely related to sharks.

Hey I'm Sean. And one animal I thought would be interesting to learn more about was the Yellowtail Snapper. Yellowtail snappers are found in coastal waters near coral reefs. They prefer sandy areas around the reef. We saw many of these fish as we snorkeled in the many reefs around the island.

Hi it's Tenzin you may remember me from my Yellow Tube Sponge page but I'm not going to be teaching you about the Yellow Tube Sponge. I'm going to teach you about the Angelfish. Did you know that there is a Queen Angelfish? Did you also know the Angelfish can camouflage by using their colors?

Hello, it's Zara again, from the Black Triggerfish & Sea Turtle pages. So I'm going to tell you some quick tiny facts about the Sergeant Major; it's subfamily is Damselfish. They live near the reefs and stay throughout their lives. The upper part of their body is yellow and they have 5 vertical bars but sometimes a faint sixth can be seen. They feed on algae, larvae, small crustaceans, and fish. Did you know that at night, they hide in coral crevices?

CHAPTER 3
ACTIONS WE TOOK

In all our projects and every place we go, we are determined to make a positive impact. In Providenciales, Turks and Caicos, as we learned about the magnitude of the plastic problem, we decided to brainstorm some plastic reduction ideas and apply them.

Each week all the families collected recyclables. The students took the recyclables to the school. We sorted everything and set aside the plastic. Then, we weighed it. We wanted to see how much our plastic use was going up or down as we applied more reduction strategies. We measured the impact of the changes we made. Here are our ideas and data (all in kgs).

Can you examine our data and figure out the difference between our plastic use weight in week 1 compared to week 3? How much did our plastic use weight go down in 4 weeks?

PLASTIC REDUCTION PHASES

Plastic Reduction Ideas Phase 1
- Refill current bottles (only for about a week)
- Buy/use reusable water bottles
- Choose brands like Evian that are made from recycled plastic
- Look for products in larger packages /bulk
- Buy biodegradable products
- Use all the food or product in the package
- Look for foods not wrapped in plastic (cucumbers, tomatoes, etc..)
- Make sure it's something you need

Plastic Reduction Ideas Phase 2
- Contact companies that sell favorite products and use high amounts of plastic
- Ask them to use new packaging that is safer for the environment
- If they have other options available ask them to make them available globally
- Offer new reduced plastic use ideas to companies
- Offer ideas to companies developing packaging for new products
- Help people become aware of the environmentally friendly products that are available

Plastic Reduction Ideas Phase 3
- When ordering food request that they do not include plastic utensils or straws and use your own
- Chose hotels that apply sustainable practices
- Donate clothing instead of throwing it away- some clothing has plastic inside it
- Contact places you plan to go and then ask to use fewer plastic bottles by removing things like disposable shampoo containers from your room, then you can bring your own

One thing we have been doing is beach clean-ups. You may think that cleaning up might not be fun, but it is. You can see so many things on the beach. For example, you can see a lot of beautiful things like shells and crabs. And maybe you will see some special things like Yellow Tube Sponges. It is fun! Do you think it would be fun? I think it would be nice if you could join us or have your own beach clean-up.

Here is the info we got from the beach clean-ups. In the first beach clean up, shown in blue, we collected less than 5 kgs. Can you tell how much we collected in the 2nd beach clean up, shown in red? Approximately how much more did we clean up in the 2nd clean up?

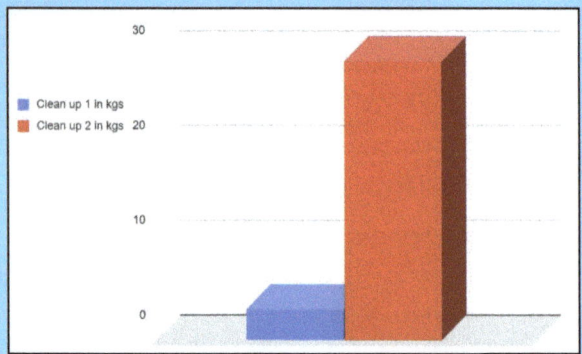

Here are some ideas from our class about other things you can do too.

- recycle
- have beach clean-ups
- pick up trash
- use things from nature in a responsible way
- conserve water
- conserve energy
- use reusable bags instead of plastic bags
- use less fertilizer
- reduce your carbon footprint
- join us in plastic free July where people all over the world don't use plastic for a month!

You may be wondering why we decided to pick up trash, recycle our own trash, and collect and weigh our plastic. Well, we learned that there are 300,000,000 tons of plastic in the ocean!!!! At first, we didn't really grasp how much that was, but we let our curiosity take us into some research and what we found shocked us. Maybe what we found will surprise you too!

To help us visualize how much plastic is in the ocean we used math to compare.

Here are some things that equal the amount of plastic in the ocean:

150,000,000,000,000 jellyfish based on a 2 kg jellyfish
100,000,000,000,000 lego kids
16,500,000,000 Tenzins (our youngest female student)
13,000,000,000 groups of our school body based on our weight of 231 kgs
75,000,000 cigarette boats (Devin's favorite 4 ton boat)
60,000,000 elephants (avg. weight)
30,000,000 school buses
125,000 olympic sized swimming pools' water
7,500 cruise ships based on a 40,000 ton ship

Do you know about place value? We looked at many numbers large and small, and realized how big some of the figures are!

Can you identify which things had to be in the billions to equal the amount of plastic in the ocean?

How many Green Sea turtles do you think would equal 300,000,000 million tons of plastic? Check out the Green Sea Turtle page to see how much they weigh.

We learned that 1 ton equals 1000 kgs and 1 kg equals 0.001 of a ton; 1 gram equals 0.001 of a kilogram and 1 kilogram equals 1000 grams. This helped us compute.

If a LEGO kid weighs 3 grams how many LEGO kids would have to be in the ocean to equal 300,000,000 tons?

If you know how much you weigh or the weight of your favorite things, you can solve problems like this too.

Our collective life-span is 133 years.

We computed that we need to live what we have lived 3 times more to come close to the average expected time it takes for a plastic bottle to decompose. Our research also taught us that this depends on the composition of the plastic and its exposure to the elements, like the sun.

Can you figure out approximately how long it takes a plastic bottle to decompose using the our collective life span and the information in the text?

Domain	Eucaryote							
Kindom	Animalia							
Phylum	Chordata							Mollusca
Class	Reptilia		Teleostei				Chonderchthyes	Malacostrancans
Order	Squamata	testudines	Beloniformes	Tetraodontiformes	Perciformes		myliobatiformes	Decapods
Family	Iguanidae	cheloniidae	Hemiramphidae	Balistidae	Labridae		Dasyatidae	Brachyura/Crab
Genus	Cyclura	Chelonia	Hemiramphus	Melichthys	Xyrichtys		Taeniura	
Species	Cyclura carinata/ Turks and Caicos rock iguana	Chelonia mydas/ Green sea turtle	Hemiramphus brasiliensis/ Ballyhoo	M. Niger/black durgon	Xyrichtys splendens/ green razorFish		Taeniura lymma/ bluespotted ribbontail ray	

Domain	Eucaryote							
Kindom	Animalia							
Phylum	Cnidaria					Porifera		Arthropods
Class	Anthoza			Scyphozoa	Hydrozoa	Demospongiae		Gastropods
Order		Scleractinia	Alcyonacea	Rhizostomae	Anthoathecata	Verongida		Neogastropoda
Family	Sea anemone	Mussidae	Gorgoniidae	Cassiopeidae	Milleporidae	Aplysiidae		Buccinidae/ whelk
Genus	Strichodactylidae	Diplora	Gorgonia/ fan coral	Cassiopea/Upside down jellifish	Millepora	Aplysina		
Species	Strichodactyla	Diploria labyrinthiformis/			Millepora dichotoma/	Fistularis/ Yellow Tube		
	Giganta/Blue carpet ananomy							

52

Below are some questions about taxonomic ranking and our cladogram. Learning about this really helped us see how everything is connected. If you examine the taxonomic rankings in our book and this cladogram, you will be able to answer these questions and learn a lot about how things are connected.

What are the similarities between the Green Sea Turtle and the Black Triggerfish?

When do you notice that the similarities end?

Do you think the Green Sea Turtle is from the Chordata or Mollusca Phylum? Do they share the same domain? If yes, what?

What is the name of the phylum of the Anemone featured in this book?

Where does the crab taxonomically connect with any other of our sea animals?

Which animal is closest to the Ballyhoo?

Which two Phylum do all of our animals fall into?

What is the Order of the Brain Coral? What other creatures are in the same Order?

What class is the Rock Iguana found in?

CHAPTER 4
MORE TO KNOW

REFERENCES

Island organics
arlenehall2011@yahoo.com

Yellowtail snapper (Ocyurus chrysurus) - Pictures and facts - Fish @ thewebsiteofeverything.com

http://awesomeocean.com/news/awesome-facts-stingrays/

https://easyscienceforkids.com/lifecycle-of-a-fish/

https://www.originaloysterhouse.com/crab-fact/

https://en.wikipedia.org/wiki/Crab

https://www.washingtonpost.com/news/morning-mix/wp/2016/11/28/scientists-discover-the-remarkable-strength-of-coconut-crabs-claws-get-pinched-in-process/

https://edition.cnn.com/2019/12/05/world/hermit-crabs-plastic-pollution-intl-scli-scn/index.html

https://www.theguardian.com/environment/2020/apr/29/microplastics-disrupt-hermit-crabs-ability-to-choose-shell-study-suggest

RESOURCES

These are resources we engaged with on our learning journey. We enjoyed non-fiction articles, documentaries, non-fiction and fiction books, youtube videos, and our own experiences in and around the ocean waters, to help us understand, appreciate, and inform on the topics in this book. We hope you take time to explore them and enjoy them too!

We also have created a YouTube channel where you will find videos of us sharing more things we learned about the ocean and you can see our rap video called "Save the Ocean". Use this link to see more cool stuff on the isy! school channel. Website coming soon! https://www.youtube.com/channel/UCgVnHJjemNi3y1SGkHQhh5w

1. Anna's World Online, author of the book we read "Microplastics" https://www.annadu.org/
2. "Deike"- AKA Devent Quant Jr. Head Grower of Caicos Acres. Deike was our guide and teacher in the mangroves, a host during Earth Day, and our friend and helper during the beach clean-ups in TCI. CAICOSACRES@GMAIL.COM
3. Bethany Stahl is "Save the Ocean" https://www.bethanystahl.com/
4. Netflix "David Attenborough Life on our Planet"
5. Netflix "Chasing Coral"
6. Netflix -"Mission Blue"
7. Netflix-- "A Plastic Ocean"
8. YouTube.com "Walt Whitman- The Early Years"
9. Amanda Goram www.theamandagorman.com

10. "Heal the Earth" by Julian Lennon
11. "Ocean Animals and Their Ecosystems" by Dr. Erica
12. "How to Make a Better World" By Keilly Swift
13. "Citizens of the Sea"- By Nancy Knowlton
14. "Microplastics and Me"- Anna Du
15. "What a Waste"- By Jess French
16. "Save the Ocean"- By Bethany Stahl
17. "Life in the Ocean The Story of Oceanographer Sylvia Earle"- By Claire A. Nivola
18. Tracking Trash"-By Loree Griffin Burns
19. "Ocean- A Visual Encyclopedia" By Smithsonian
20. "A Children's Encyclopedia of Ocean Life"- Claudia Martin
21. Fisker Ocean- A car that is made with caring for the ocean in mind https://www.fiskerinc.com
22. "Plant A Million Corals"- Dr. David Vaughn www.plantamillioncorals.org
23. "New plant-based plastics can chemically recycle with near perfect efficiency:- www.academictimes.com
24. "Kenyan Woman Invents Machine that Turns Plastic into Paving Blocks" By "In The Know" https://www.intheknow.com/
25. "Our Blue Planet: Accidental Discovery Could Save Coral Reefs" By BBC
26. https://newsela.com/read/elem-cc-napoleon-wrasse/id/34903/
27. https://newsela.com/read/great-barrier-reef-sun-shield/id/41887/
28. https://newsela.com/read/natgeo-symbiosis/id/47198/
29. www.oceana.org
30. www.oceancleanup.com
31. http://evolvingsciences.com
32. www.tfhmagazine.com

GLOSSARY

Antimicrobials - something that Yellow Tube Sponges make to help cure cancer.

Breed - mate and then produce offspring.

Buoyant - something that floats.

Catastrophe - an event causing great and often sudden damage or suffering; a disaster.

Consensus - a general agreement.

Commission - a group formed to do a specific kind of work

Copepods - a small or microscopic aquatic crustacean of the large class Copepoda.

Consumers - a person or thing that eats or uses something.

Decompose - to break down

Ecosystem - a biological community of interacting organisms and their physical environment.

Endangered - a species seriously at risk of extinction

Expedition - a journey undertaken by a group of people with a particular purpose, especially that of exploration, research, or war.

Fragile - easily broken or damaged.

Gyre - large system of circulating ocean currents; gyres are caused by the coriolis effect among other natural forces.

Habitat - A natural home or environment of animals, plants, or other organisms

Offspring - an animal's young

Omnivores - an animal or person that eats food of both plant and animal origin.

Predator - they eat other animals.

Preserve - maintain or keep-alive

Sandblasting - roughen or clean a surface with a jet of sand driven by compressed air.

Taxonomic - concerned with the classification of things, especially organisms.

Vegetation - plants considered collectively, especially those found in a particular area or habitat

Invertebrates - do not have a backbone

Osculum - a big hole on the top of the Yellow Tube Sponge

Sessile - can not move

Spawn - leave eggs to be fertilized

Zooplankton - plankton consisting of small animals and the immature stages of larger animals.

ABOUT THE AUTHORS

Hi my name is Sean Madan. I am eight years old and I love coming to Turks and Caicos. My family visits these beautiful islands every winter. I love water sports but I still don't know all of them and this is the perfect place to learn. I also love math and science!!! I love this place and I think it could be 100 times better than what it is now if everyone does their part to help.

Hi my name is Devin Madan I am 6 years old. My hobbies are building things and enjoying nature. Turks and Caicos are special to my family because we like the ocean and we come here every year.

Hi my name is Zara Bhushan. I Love drawing and eating ice cream. I really enjoy the ocean! I came to visit Turks and Caicos to vacation with my family and friends.

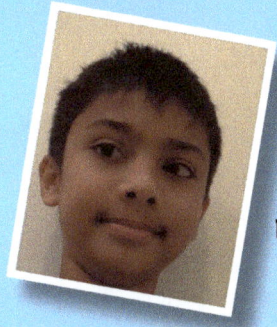

HI my name is Sai. I love to code, eat and save the planet. This is my first time in Turks and Caicos, but not on an island paradise.

Hi, my name is Tenzin. I am 6.5 years old and I like nature and love to do art. It is fun! I am on vacation in Turks and Caicos!

Hi, I'm Kavi Bhushan. I am 6 years old and I like to play LEGO with my sister Zara and my brother Sai.

My name is Alexandra Macare. I am a lifelong learner passionate about inspiring others to live their lives learning. I enjoy nature and collaborating with young people to broaden their knowledge and experience the interconnectedness of life.

My name is Tarsha Benevento. I am a lifelong educator and learner who is passionate about working with children and helping them find their magic I enjoy learning alongside my students every day!

SPECIAL CONTRIBUTORS

We want to thank Kian and Zaiden Chheda for being special contributors to our global message of making the world a better place. We have collaborated with them in beach clean-ups and in the production of our ocean rap! Thank you.

Hi my name is Kian. I love reading, swimming, surfing and hugging puppies. This is my first time in Turks and Caicos and I love it here!

Hi my name is Zaiden. I love swimming, riding my bike and playing with my brother. This is my first time in Turks and Caicos!

PICTURES WE TOOK

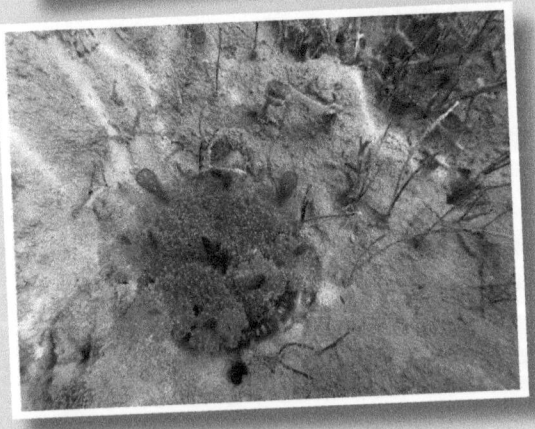

MORE POETRY FROM US

If we want to fight we will need all our might in spite of anything that might be in our way.

If we help to save the environment we might just save ourselves.

Cause At the end of the day we are all the same. even if we appear to differ we are still in this together. Help endure through this night to find the light within us all.

If we all find our light we can help brighten the way into the fog that is the future.

If we try to see into the fog we will only blind ourselves to the possibilities it provides.

Do not let the future die or else possibilities will not arise.

If possibilities do not arise the future dies and its life.

For you see they are the same for all of eternity.

The same is true for symbiosis if one of them dies the other shall never rise even if it tries.

By Sai Bhushan

Ocean I admire your ebb and flow
You remind me that
life has a purposeful tempo

Ocean I learn from your predictable directions
that waste left unattended
Will build in areas of stagnation

Ocean when I observe the power of your waves
crashing against the rocks
I see how steadily time allows everything to change

Ocean I feel your salt water tears pour from my own eyes
As the life inside you dies
Profoundly aware of life's dependency on all you supply

Ocean I see your beauty and hear you melody
And seek to know how
The generations to come will enjoy your enchanting mystery

By- Alexandra Macare